COLLECTION OF POEMS

LIFE AND DEATH AND HOLY IN EVERY BREATH

CHRISTINE SALKIN DAVIS

Wild Rising Press

EVERGREEN, COLORADO

Published by:
WILD RISING PRESS

All artwork by Christine Salkin Davis
Book Design: Mary M Meade
Editor: Judyth Hill

ISBN 978-1957468-28-0

For Kelli

Contents

Plot Twist

Coffins Crying Tears of Blood

The Drop Back to Earth After Dreams Disappear

Life and Death in Every Breath

Holy in Every Breath

Ripening

LIFE AND
DEATH
AND HOLY
IN EVERY
BREATH

Plot Twist

PLOT TWIST § NOW YOU REVEAL NEW THINGS TO
ME § THE NICU § IN THE NICU § "NANA TE AMO"
§ SONNET OF DOUBT § BABY BREATH SONNET
§ NO WORDS

PLOT TWIST

I arrived expecting full-term, healthy twins,
expecting I would change diapers and do laundry.

Instead, I hold my fragile grandson,
surviving twin of an early delivery, tragic circumstances,
praying for whatever health and happiness I can will for him.

I am grieving this loss of my grandson, of holding him in my
    arms, feeding him, changing his diapers, playing with him.

I am grieving this loss of my dreams of being there at his delivery,
    seeing him born, cutting his umbilical cord, holding him.

I am grieving this opportunity to hold two babies, one in each
    arm, overflowing with infant love.

I am grieving this sadness of his parents, loss of the pure joy—un-
    tainted with sorrow—they waited months—years—to arrive. I
    am grieving their inability to take their babies home,
their having to wait hours to see either of their babies, having to
    wait a day to hold them.

I am grieving the narrative breach. Life wasn't supposed to hap-
    pen this way.

I've forgotten how
grief feels like a sucker punch,
makes you remember,
makes you forget.

Suddenly my work seems so far away; my hands, formerly focused on writing about data and instructions, now softly stroke my grandson's soft skin.

Time stills as I hold him in my arms, smell his sweet baby smell, feel his head's weight, watch his eyelids droop heavily.

Tiny one,
I wish for you a life
as sweet as chocolate milk,
smooth as pages of a book,
warm as hot tea in cold hands,
gentle as a kitten's tongue,
as long as a day spent waiting.

I hold his bottle and watch him breathe.

NOW YOU REVEAL NEW THINGS TO ME

I feel your breath,
new,
like sun rising over Montserrat,
learning how to be alive.

I smell your softness,
new,
scent of discovering
who you are on this
blue orb turning,
blackened universe.

I see your smile,
bowed lips
turning upward,
pin dots of joy, chubby cheeks.
I hear your wail,
first of many
announcing
you.

I watch you create new memories:
  strong hands holding,
  soft breasts cradling,
  nipples feeding.

Browns, grays,
blues, yellows
swaddle you;
warm luminescent light
bathes you in love.

THE NICU

Borderland
between womb, world,
a chrysalis,
budded rose,
slow, soft blossoming.

Remedial instruction for life.
> *Lesson 1:*
>> *how to cry for comfort.*
> *Lesson 2:*
>> *how to coo for food.*

As your eyesight forms you learn shapes.
As your hearing emerges you learn voices.

You create memory pathways
of hot, cold,
pain, softness,
milk, mucus,

all a wonder
to you.

IN THE NICU

Handwash ritual,
acrid smell of antiseptic.
Please, my silent prayer.

"NANA TE AMO"

Images of babies.

Soft skin,
sleepy eyes,
smells of powder and poop,
sweet earthy smells,
rose-spotted cheeks,
perfect lips,
tiny tiny toes.

Soft head of dark hair
against caramel skin,
deep blue-gray eyes.

You weigh heavy on my chest
as you breathe,
deeply,
twitch in your dreams of
heaven, earth,
secure in your soul's memories,
trusting in this life into which you have been placed.

I hold you in my arms,
my grandson;
I give you promises of
love, safety, hope, joy, health.
Knowing I can guarantee none of these.
Te amo, mi nieto.

SONNET OF DOUBT

The horsefly buzzes around my head, takes quick
jabs near my eyes, I lose my step,

                            stumble,
shaking my head like a cow's tail in midtwitch;
they swarm, I swat at the air.

                           I grumble

at my hesitancy. I mumble
to myself,
        If god exists, why are there horseflies?
Why do people hate so much, why troubles,
pandemic, greed, why did my grandson have to die?

If god exists, I wonder if she hides
in election years and Superbowl seasons.

I wonder if she ever even tries
to smite the bad guys, if she has a reason
for babies in cages and war,

                        why this fear

in the back of my throat;

                     why this buzzing in my ear?

BABY BREATH SONNET

Sound of baby's breath replaces
monitor's beep-beep-beep,
heart sounds needed to keep
him alive, counting beats, traces of

breath-by-breath graces,
prayers over his crèche,
watching those signals for his next heartbeat,
willing that his body life embraces.

These things my heart knows to be:
optimistic partial sun of an Irish sky,
softness of a steady rain set in for days,

scraggly branches of a fairy hawthorn tree,
comfort of a baby's cry.
Beneath a crunch of leaves, new life emerges from decay.

NO WORDS

I have seen people die of broken hearts,
grief consume,
breath by breath by breath, suffocate.

I have seen loss remove reason,
ability to discern good from evil,
for all looks evil in dark void of emptiness.

I have seen death suck a mother's soul,
break a father,
sister,
brother;
I have seen words unable to comprehend.

I have seen death steer a mother into her grave,
into her black hole of anti-matter, anti-life,
when living hurts too much to bear.

I have seen a mother die of a broken heart,
night by night by night by night by night.

I have seen an altar waiting for a sign.

Coffins Crying Tears of Blood

RESURRECTION § LIFE AND DEATH AND HOLY
IN EVERY BREATH § HUNTERS AND HUNTED
§ DISAPPOINTING PLOTLINES § LOST LOVE
OPPORTUNITIES § LIMINAL FEAR STATES §
SOME NUMBERS DON'T COUNT § LAMENT TO
EVACUEES § ELEGY FOR AMERICA § RACHEL
WEEPING FOR HER CHILDREN § FIRST DAY
AFTER THE SCHOOL SHOOTING § SECOND
DAY AFTER THE SCHOOL SHOOTING § FIFTH
DAY AFTER THE SCHOOL SHOOTING § EIGHTH
DAY AFTER THE SCHOOL SHOOTING

RESURRECTION

Deep, down, really, what does this all mean,
ritualistic sun rising, moon waning, coffee drinking, holy
    communion,
resurrected secret hopes and dreams?

Whitewashed stones, lilies,
hallelujah trumpet sounds,
wake the dead in me.

Light your fire of miraculous life after life after life,
show me a connection,
then, here, now, let

truth sprigs emerge
from the ashes. Feed this flame;
justice, buried, calls,

killed,
because oxygen at the bottom is insufficient
to sustain life.

LIFE AND DEATH AND HOLY
IN EVERY BREATH

Corralled like cattle, bodies, extreme
oppressive heat, dirty, disenfranchised,
isolated, stench, despised, traumatized,
sick, afraid, inhumane, unseemly
bodies, thrown away, like meat, obscene
bodies, sweat, life and death and holy in
every dirty labored breath, bodies, din
of murmurations, bodies, let them be,
bodies, hungry, lack of humanity,
bodies, thirsty, hatred, lies, decomposed,
bodies, legacy of platitudes, disposed,
bodies, dehumanized, routinely,
bodies, separated, called unclean,
bodies, shameful. This is our history.

HUNTERS AND HUNTED

(Upon visiting Montgomery, Alabama's Legacy Museum;
National Memorial for Peace and Justice;
Civil Rights Memorial and Center)

I am among the daughters of fate; hunters and hunted.

The sins of our fathers' bodies lay the shame in ours.
Their voices ghostly, hard to hear—we listen
to the ones born, bound, and died in the shackles of hate.

The numbers speak: Twelve million kidnapped.

I feel it in my body; in the knot in the pit of my stomach, the
    breath struggling to escape from my throat.
The numbers speak: Anthony Ray Hinton spent 30 years on
    death row for a crime he did not commit.
Whites only!
    Whites only!
        Whites only!
            Whites only!
                Whites only!
                    Whites only!
                        Whites.
                            Only.
The numbers speak: Twenty-four thousand enslaved.
Bravely waiting for God.
A people shaped by slavery. We are all shaped by slavery.

The sins of our fathers' bodies lay the shame in ours,
born, bound, and died in the shackles of hate.

I dreamed we were the ones stripped bare, shackled by shame.

You feel it in your body; in the knot in the pit of your stomach,
   the breath that struggles to escape from your throat.
Anthony Ray Hinton asks *what would you do?* What would you
   do if they came for you? What would you do? You.
Whites only!
   Whites only!
      Whites only!
         Whites only!
            Whites only!
               Whites only!
                  Whites.
                     Only.
From dust we came, to dust we will all return.

Bravely waiting for God.
Waiting still.
I hear my daughter, but I can't find her.
   I can't find her.
      I can't find her.
A people shaped by slavery. We are all shaped by slavery.

Have you seen our mother?
   Mother?
      Mother?

Waiting waiting waiting for the day of God's retribution. Waiting
   still.
I dreamed we were stripped bare, shackled by shame.
Is anyone ever free from the river of blood?

The numbers speak:
Anthony Ray Hinton spent 30 years on death row for a crime he
   did not commit.
These coffins crying tears of blood.

From dust we came, to dust we will all return,
lined up and hanging,
say their names:
Ed White, lynched June 25, 1894, in Lamar County, Alabama.
This is not a poem of absolution.

I hear my daughter, but I can't find her.
    I can't find her.
Have you seen our mother?
    Mother?

The numbers speak: Twenty-four thousand enslaved.

Waiting waiting waiting for the day of God's retribution. Waiting
    still.

Their voices ghostly, hard to hear, but listen.
Is anyone ever free from the river of blood?
You are among the daughters of fate; hunters and hunted.

Coffins crying tears of blood.
Anthony Ray Hinton asks *what would you do*? What would we do
    if they came for us?
What would we do? Us.
Our brothers and sisters, lined up and hanging,
say their names:
John Boggan, lynched July 3, 1885, in Anson County, North
    Carolina.

This is not a poem of absolution.
The numbers speak: Twelve million kidnapped.

The numbers speak: Twenty-four thousand enslaved.
We feel it in our bodies; in the knot in the pit of our stomachs,

the breath that struggles to escape from our throats.
Bravely waiting for God.

The numbers speak:
Anthony Ray Hinton spent 30 years on death row for a crime he
    did not commit.

I hear my daughter, but I can't find her.
    I can't find her.
Waiting waiting waiting for the day of God's retribution.
    Waiting still.

Their voices, ghostly, hard to hear, but listen.
Is anyone ever free from the river of blood?

We are among the daughters of fate; hunters and hunted,
calling the names on coffins crying tears of blood.

Say their names.

Thomas Johnson, lynched May 29, 1898, in Cabarrus County,
    North Carolina.

Samuel Arline, lynched April 14, 1912, in Hillsborough County,
    Florida.

Clinton Melton, lynched December 3, 1955, in Glendora,
    Mississippi.

Anthony Ray Hinton spent 30 years on death row for a crime he
    did not commit.

This is not a poem of absolution.

DISAPPOINTING PLOTLINES

The veil of illusions has lifted, and
we're all just one disappointment away
from a breakdown. Possibilities, plans
gone awry. My frustrating plot displays

misplaced trust in today's fair world. To stand
is to hope, but things aren't going the way
of goodness or roses. It's this dreamland
that lets you down. Humanity betrays

us in her ignorance, hateful arrogance.
The distance between two lost souls is vast;
our cocoon of sameness a hindrance
to understanding. Resentments amassed;

yet, this bird sings in the midst of the rain.
I want her eyes to see instead of mine.

LOST LOVE OPPORTUNITIES

As bad news, overwhelming sadness overtake you, suffocating
heaviness of non-stop rain for weeks, you wonder, when will earth
finally awaken, her blossoms blooming, bursting out in nature's
crush on herself? You look for a glimmer of light in the headlines
but instead, those haters have won another round, doors slammed
shut against themselves.

As you attempt to dig yourself out of this avalanche of disillusion,
you feel adrift. This has been a week of opportunities, lost, for
love to show her face. Alas,

love does not appear to be winning these
days. Separation, isolation, you
can dress up in fancy clothes, but, please,
rejection still stings. The news,

earth-quaking, foundation-shaking sleaze,
disappointments, rock my world. Look at
the sky, weeping tears. Like a refugee
to people who seem to care about you

from people who clearly don't, you're feeling
hurt. Missed connections, misconceptions,
missed opportunities to love. Kneeling,
will this month ever end? Perceptions,

field-day fears, dreams in my mind. My
coracle has sailed, I look for skies

of blue, but I'm a bit seasick at the first gust of wind, like saints,
sailing without a rudder.

You search for gratitude for what you have lost, compassion for those who never had it in the first place. Trust that all this rain feeds an abundance of flowers.

LIMINAL FEAR STATES

Afraid to leave, afraid to stay,
liminal fear states, the only way out
goes through.

Shake this dust from your feet
when you walk by.
Faith? Hope? Love?

Rage is the new faith.
Hiding behind the cross;
protected by power.

This body built by shame.
Layers of shame.
You told us if we were good girls

you would protect us.
You lied.
You once erased me;

I will no more be silent.
She waited until it felt safe;
courage is the new safe.

SOME NUMBERS DON'T COUNT

in response to the news headline
"Trump Claims Without Evidence that
3,000 People Did Not Die in Puerto Rico Hurricanes,
Blames Democrats for Inflating Toll"

Three thousand people dead from incompetence,
indifference; their lives don't count,

didn't count then, don't count now—the
"collective black," too dark to be seen
in the black pit of our collective soul.

The transformation starts with your eyes
wide open. Count them now before
no one is left to count.

LAMENT TO EVACUEES

Toppled by hurricane hype of the hour,
red-arrowed bubbled maps pointing
circuitous path of destruction, mayhem; their dour
pronouncements, minute by minute spent waiting

reach their climax in fizzles, turns, news
of nothing, as your attention gets sharper, better,
slipping by still unheeded one other doom—
while storm evacuees refuge in shelters,

12,000 migrant children, held, detained,
callous indifference our collective soul, stained.

ELEGY FOR AMERICA

The deaths of children as weapons of war.
Desperate people do desperate things.
Their hearts beat, then they didn't anymore.

Say her name, Jakelin, seven, she died for
nothing? Whatever racism brings.
Deaths of children as weapons of war.

Say his name, Darlyn, he was adored.
People don't leave if they have anything.
His heart beat, then didn't anymore.

He had a home, then didn't anymore.
Say his name, Carlos, now on angel wings.
Deaths of children as weapons of war.

Say his name, Felipe, eight; you know his death tore
his family; Wilmer, two, his death also stings.
Their hearts beat, then didn't anymore.

Say his name, Juan de León, no more.
Desperate people do desperate things.
Deaths of children as weapons of war.
Their hearts beat, then didn't anymore.

RACHEL WEEPING FOR HER CHILDREN

I am haunted by her face,
this mother, breasts heavy with milk,
arms heavy with ghosts of her child,
belly swollen from months of carrying love.

Her face, as they ripped her child,
literally,
from her breast,
frozen in a millisecond of disbelief,
her heart breaking in two,
her cries so loud I can hear them half a world away.
Can you hear her cries in the wind?

Raped, beaten, threatened, starved,
she crossed 500 miles of dangerous desert
for our land of refuge,
now a house of horrors.

Rachel weeping for her children.
I weep in gratitude my forefathers cannot see what we have
   become.

FIRST DAY AFTER THE SCHOOL SHOOTING

How do they take their exams, deciding
their future, with their heart still pounding, fear
in their throats, frantic mem'ries, surviving
(some did not) a meeting with Death, terror
storming the mind, the test faced now appears,
our collective test, the only fact we
must learn, forty-thousand dead last year
from guns, breathtaking, can you guarantee
my students they will not die today, me
that my next lecture will not be my last,
war zone, hell on earth, no one, nobody,
should fear they will be shot sitting in class.
As I breathe in the aftermath of death,
I fear the holy has escaped with their breath.

SECOND DAY AFTER THE SCHOOL SHOOTING

How can rustling trees dance their wild dance,
shimmering leaves, birdsong symphony;
how can sunshine in the sky take a chance,
when not yet buried in the grave is he?

How can butterflies fly so carefree,
how can trees still stand, earth still turn,
how can clouds float across the sky, lazy,
when mourners have not begun to mourn?

Why don't meetings, work, email, adjourn?
I need some space, time to pause today.
I'm drowning in emotions and concerns.
I need to not have to know what to say.

I do know I will have to find a way,
but I'm a little raw right now to start.
So can't I wait until a better day?
I skinned my knee, only it was my heart.

FIFTH DAY AFTER THE SCHOOL SHOOTING

Some may say world's end occurred that night.
Yet, I awake. Life persists after all.
Sunrise encroaches on darkness, first light,
as day, in turn, always ends at nightfall,

stars shine enough, night sky overhaul.
Dusk, meditation, gin blurs the eyes—
whatever helps you survive this downfall
from sameness, safety, I empathize—

stare into hate long enough, spirit dies.
Can't our hearts break; feel the grief, feel the pain;
in the decay's where resurrection lies.
Our world ended that night in a heart stain.

Holiest of holies sometimes speaks
in whispers. Or wails of distress, tear streaks.

EIGHTH DAY AFTER THE SCHOOL SHOOTING

It's called *mortality salience*.

I know, I study this stuff.

It's anxiety tightening around my eyes as
I see campus for the first time since,
looking into eyes bloodshot in exhausted faces,
tears at their corners,
bodies falling in our fretful sleep.

I scan the paper, we are yesterday's news,
students shot dead in classrooms are everyday sights.

Mortality salience.
I scan the landscape for last week's memorial flowers on the
     schoolhouse steps;
the steps lie bare.

Ghostly memories of last week's lit white candles lingers;
the classroom building itself, a visual monument to death.

Everywhere I look, a reminder.
These eyes remember what they didn't see.

Mortality salience.
The picture in the back of my eyeballs haunts.

Unexpectedly traveling too close to the edge,
looking down.

The Drop Back to Earth After Dreams Disappear

STORMS

Last night's thunderstorm, incarnation
of angry power, storms of life stop you in
your tracks. Sleepwalk until crash awakens
you, fear overtakes you, you can't move.

Eventually, your thinking improves.
But this sudden flash, in my opinion,
of lightning, hurts less than this forsaken
drip, drip, drip, drip daily deluge

of rain, bad news, disappointments, dead
ends, terminal delays, like stepping
in a deep puddle while a car, spraying
you with water, speeds by. Fills me with dread;

when a steady drizzle sets in for days,
it's hard to trust the sun will return again.

SONNET OF PRAISE

Praise be to divine disappointments,
doubts, broken dreams. So close I can feel
your holy breath, soft voice in my ear,
shadows on a cloudy day. Praise too, to contentment,

holy puffy clouds, blue skies, sunlight poignant
on disappointing days, sky who gives, steals
back ones who almost were. Praise be to the year
with its scent of rotten bananas or yesterday's ointment,

leaves turning gold, crimson, final
show of ostentatious beauty before
falling in a heap on the forest floor. Praise be

to holy harvest moons, their primal
pull. Praise be to seeds in blackest soil.
Praise be to spring blossoms which from darkness reap.

YOUR SONNET

I wish for you a love that takes your breath away.
On you to shine the morning sun; songbirds to sing
to you. I wish much happiness breaks through today,
a sparkling rainbow sky many lilies to you bring,

so many that they form an extravagant bouquet.
I wish you find the fearless life you want; take wing,
explore delight. (I love your tender heart—the way
your kindness soothes like a gently flowing spring.)

I wish your sunsets rise, pink pushing off the gray
sky streaks into a daybreak song that plucks heartstrings,
yellow-orange harpsichord, conspicuous display,
sunflower hues, one starry night, blue iris fling

for miles. I wish you peace of million midnight moons,
scents of honeysuckle summer nights in June.

MOONLIGHT SONNET

In the light of the sliver of moon,
comfort from its hazy glow, eerie trace
of vapor sky bound, vastness, stars full bloom,
silence, breathless silence, in this place.

In joyful, rapt attention, I'm consumed;
stillness, stillness, airy breathless space.
I grasp the darkness, wraps me like a womb;
blackening night surrounds me in embrace.

Blood red, wounded, pain, collective pain,
weeping wails cry out into the night.
Dusky silence, agony of heartstain
pierces the peace, unsettled, 'til morning light.

They'd fill an ocean, tears we all have shed.
No one has peace in shadows of the dead.

PONDERINGS

Maybe that free-fall sensation is you
floating in the ocean, love, divine, hold.
Maybe darkness is the way through,
releasing your fears to lighten your load.

Cleansing power of the black silky moon,
you're under its spell, deep night sky, cold.
Bright white stars, pinpricks in velvety view,
glimpses, shining radiantly bold.

Maybe when you're lost you can look for truth
in words the ancestors foretold.
Maybe chaos yields a breakthrough
breaking the surface, secrets exposed.

Welcome your ashes, wounded deity,
be where you are, then be where you will be.

BE BRAVE

Flash of cardinal red amid wet
dreary winter, birdsongs drowned out by rain.
Drops drip in streaks upon the windowpane,
pocks of puddles in the storm-soaked lawn. Yet,

hints of blue peek out, as if they met
blackened clouds en route to earth, came
to save us. Birds chase the air, their rain-stained
feathers flying to the treetops, buoyant

avigation. Early signs of spring's sight.
You ponder rhymes to speak on paper, ink
blots blooming flowers, sunshine, painting pink
pictures on the page, portal to heart's light.

You know those words that terrify you? Be
brave. Secrets spoke aloud will set you free.

DREAMS

Midnight blue, crescent moon, black tree-
tops in silhouette below. Velvet sky
falls. I am a bird banging against the
windowpane, dimly lit. Away I fly.

Breeze blows leaves in field strewn yellowed wheat.
They dance, dash in frenzied battle cry.
I too am trapped by winds of fortune; freed
in dreams, storied visions passing by.

The cherry tree's in bloom, past winter's chill,
robin's wings emerge as feath'ry gust.
Inside, the fire warms my heart, stills
disquiet of my soul; return I must

to pictures painted on a page in black
ink wand'rings; riding letters forth and back.

WHEN

after Wendell Berry

When I sit among trees,
watch dying dogwood's leaves curl
in frilly edge like lips pursed around a lemon wedge;

when I feel forlorn
under a graying sky,
summer storms ahead;

when my sandals stick in a hydrogen haze,
when Picasso might have painted my day;
when I'm living a series of whole notes on Mars,
when air smells of nothing but decay,

birds sing off-key,
flying bugs tickle my skin,

I sip my coffee,
creamy tart, smooth edge on soft lips,
warmth on tongue,

wait for the gust I know will arrive,
a caress, a softness blowing in.

DEFAULT TO LIFE

Heartbeats, now measured heart-to-heart;
my arms ache from unfamiliar weight,
arms that recently ached from its lack.

You can feel the season changing,
moon's darkness into a new day morn.
The first golden leaf appears, then another.

Three plants survived the summer storms.
One proudly raises her lush leaves, blossoms, to the sky.
One has a wild look of a boxer after winning a tough fight.

The last, beaten down in defeat, prostrated,
lone red flower stretches up from dragging debris.
She is my favorite, reaching for one more shot at the sun, grasping
    for life.

A robin flies, blue peeks through the clouds,
sounds still,
breeze rustles the trees.

I BELIEVE

I believe the beauty of a sunset makes you cry.
I believe the majesty of moon and stars
brings light into your darkest night,
each sunrise holds one thousand more.

I believe in life-givingness of trees,
dogs, magic spells of words on page.
I believe the holy lies in crunching leaves,
bodies aching with exertion of age.

This, this, the only thing that matters:
cleaning vomit from a loved one's lips,
holding a hand for a life in tatters.
A steaming latte in a china cup

shared with a friend, the sweetness of a just-
washed baby, these remain things you can trust.

DANCING IN THE DARK

after Bill Holm

I sway to birdsong backbeat,
childhood games' memories,
drizzling drops—
a rhythmic foundation to my nighttime fantasies.

A harp plays,
sparrow incessantly sings,
maybe a whip-poor-will,
still,
a song.

Maybe it's Sophia,
music of the muse,
poet,
joy from within.

A full moon,
also my heart,
as the ant
industriously studies the coffee stain on my poetry page.

Shadows gaze down,
haze,
from clouds above,
gray,
music, 3-beat Strauss waltz,
she dances in time,
her own time.

She dances in the dark,
music plays loudly,

blueberry sweet,
soft kiss memory,
wistfully swaying, violin swells,
crescendo.

The ant, gone,
blue jay carries the tune,
silence.

PARABLE OF THE SEED

Beneath paving stones, an occasional weed
pokes through dried dirt, weathered remnants of debris.

I step, gray gravel-filled hexagon crunches.
Tendrils, emerging stems, curl. One stone touches

another. Dirt, moss, hardened earth lie under
browning vegetation, stumped, nearby blunder.

A lone heart-shaped leaf tittups, blowing breeze, green,
reaching. Flowing ivy-covered trees, buds glean

vining leaves as they bypass the soil below.
Thin tricolored carpet, ostentatious show,

verdure shoots shorn exactly three inches deep.
Closer inspection reveals straw-colored heaps

flattened underfoot, moss growing, thickened base,
graceful arching form, floating, dancing grass blades.

Dark wooded decay fills deep crevices made
by irregular shapes of stones, quartz, blue-gray-

brown patterns on rocks form a smooth painterly
surface of lines, curves, an effect praiseworthy.

Seeds scatter wildly, a later winter composts
solitude. Sublime silence soothes the watery ghost.

SEASON OF GOODBYE

From time to time to timelessness,
emergent light of broken beings,
light, dark, a shadow's rest,
death, life, in-between.

Shadows form a third dimension,
flashes like lightning fill the sky,
bright-filled glimpses from the tension,
this, a season of goodbye.

Sorrow hides like ghosts in shadows,
ready at random times to pounce,
outer signs of inward struggles
call you to their two-step dance.

Pose questions to the darkness,
find your answers in its silence.

MORE

After Moya Cannon

And more comes to us.
Just when you stop searching,
think decay has ended,
more comes to us,
flowering weeds,
what you thought died
returns with a word,
and more,
searching for beauty in the white space between,
a spark comes to us,
a pink flower,
a ladybug,
a blue sky beyond,
a breeze, a calm,
peace comes to us
when you stop searching for more.

All, this bug caught in the web;
All, our own prey.

LONGEST NIGHT OF THE YEAR

Longest night of the year,
black sky, pelting rain,
asphalt dark save reflections of red brake lights,
distorted view for a missing faith,

blackness, glare advancing.
Reason, rumination
cannot fix navigational lostness,
neon confusion,

searching for a sign that means something.
A center circles with centripetal force,
you sojourn in the mess.

But the birds sing,
breeze blows,
grass grows brown,
your dog sleeps at your feet.

 **ife & Death in Every Breath**

HAIBUN OF DISAPPOINTMENTS § ODE TO THE RUNNING SHOE § HIDDEN COLORS § START AT THE HEART § I AM § I DO NOT LOVE YOU § IS IT A SECRET IF EVERYONE KNOWS IT BUT NO ONE TALKS ABOUT IT? § LAMENT TO TIME § HOLDING ON TO THE THINGS I LOVE § MOTHER WOUND § SEASON'S ROULETTE § WE ALWAYS WISH § THE MUTE PRINCESS § SHE § WITHOUT COMPROMISE

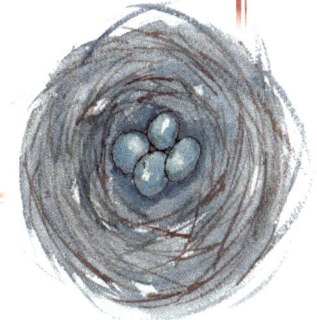

HAIBUN OF DISAPPOINTMENTS

Morning starts with a flurry of phone calls. I don't know how to translate my feelings into words,

confused, frustrated,
out of ink, out of plans,
floundering, alone,

save me from this skin crawling with impatience, fitting too tight, mind suddenly seeing what I don't want to see, crooked pictures, memories skewed, too many hands grasping at me,

maybe I don't know
what I know, then what? This may
not be the rock you

think you stand on,

sunlight in your eyes reflects a prism of colors that disappear in the darkness, maybe darkness illuminates the really real.

Sometimes you must face
a vision head-on, into
eyes of truth—Look!

at the real—bodies decaying, wearing out, faltering steps in the march to the end, shorter than before, grasping at safety, slippery touch,

dreams, loss,
the drop back to earth after
dreams disappear.

ODE TO THE RUNNING SHOE

The closet, darkened.

Lying obsolete in the back
corner a Nike shoe, stalled,

her mate under bedsheets strewn
on the floor, paralyzingly glued
since the fall. The distance from bed to ground,

a million miles and steep downhill.
Stuck still like a stop in the middle

of the street. Like miscreants locked
up, wagtail's morning song out of

reach, jigsaw pieces stirred,
waiting for reassembly.

Time, stilled.

HIDDEN COLORS

I rush past this black and white world, snapshots holding their
breath in their invisible orbs. Rain pelts my umbrella as I struggle
to balance my backpack, lunch bag, phone, life, trying to mini-
mize wet papers, frizzy hair, exhaustion, rushing to my car, feeling
energy of a slug washed up at my feet,

first-day-back energy,

blood-red energy, color of frenetic breath,
my heart echoes in emptiness.

Make the most of the shift,
embrace busy-ness, activity, movement,
buzzing adrenaline,
return to doing.

Time for contemplation passed,
now, action.

Not a week to dive deep,
rather glide the surface, hold on.

Save commentary,
philosophical ponderings for
another day.

Today, verdant green,
color of growth, wildness,
cover my nakedness with illusionary tactics.
Your neat little order frays already, outside the lines, spilling over,
    recklessness, disorder transgressing.

Sift out essential essence,
hold on, but gently.

Remember,
you have grounded.
Time to take flight.

Rebalance the load.

Sing the song you were meant to sing;
it will find its tune as you go.

Sing blue, the color of sky, of flight, of day.

START AT THE HEART

There's nothing like waking up to the sound of a sick dog hacking, pitter-patter of doggy feet circling the tile floor, to start your day with adrenaline surging, heart racing, breath catching. Your eyes automatically look for vomit on the floor before you step.

Start at the feet.
Let love flow from the ground
to the heart; stay true
in the moment.

The vet says it's the pneumonia in her lungs breaking up, a good-news phase, but I have to take that on faith. She sounds terrible, deep lung coughs, raspy, rough, that catch in my throat, hurt just to listen to her. She looks awful, yellow bile on the floor, head hanging down, shoulders hunched. Her big brown eyes look up at me. My heart breaks for her.

Start at the heart,
the beat, in this place, time,
of humility—humanity,
extend the compassion.

She lies on the floor—appetite gone from the meds—while I spoon-feed her a few yogurt bites, only thing she will eat this morning, turning her nose up at spoonfuls of pureed pears, peas, sweet potatoes, chicken.

Start at the eyes,
place of deepest bonds, extend
touch, release breath,
embrace good.

Now she lies peacefully at my feet, morning meds kicking in, eyes closed, breathing softly.

Start with the breath,
be a refuge, a conduit for miracles.
As earth erodes under your feet,
opportunity for love.

I AM

I am a quiet listener in the silence of a late-night house.

I am a new moon hope, full moon fruition.

I am a silky gliding pen on paper,
mouth eager for my first sip of morning coffee
steaming smooth lip of this homemade mug.

I am a tree frog croaking in inky darkness,
gust of stars, lavender sweet.

I am a quarter note in a Wagner opera,
awkwardly dancing to "Hey Jude,"
"Let it Be."

I am a 2 a.m. semicolon;
golden glint in winter Alps,
random Tuesday in March.

I am as heavy as chalk dust
ready as a suitcase waiting to be unpacked.

I am whatever wind blows through chimes on a hot July day.

I DO NOT LOVE YOU

after Neruda

I do not love you like a breathy vowel,
or a pearl, or a blood-red rose.
I love you like green shoots of weeds
emerging in flowerpots of dead leaves, decaying debris.

I love you like a midnight dream
in a Little Dipper sky
snuggled under a soft comforter on a cold winter's night.
You, my *ring around the rosie* rhyme.

My love is pewter, an ellipsis,
a constant tapping in my ear.
I love you like summer-day sameness
in a long-lived life sameness.

My love, long breaths, heartbeats slow,
blue jay swooping in from flight,
maybe even an artichoke at night,
or the pale sleep of a misanthrope.

IS IT A SECRET IF EVERYONE KNOWS IT BUT NO ONE TALKS ABOUT IT?

after Nâzim Hikmet

I never knew I loved your continual chat chat chat
bringing my morning coffee
in my Carolina blue mug,
reflecting the sky.

I never knew I loved kenopsia,
soul's solitude,
an echo off the River Liffey Bridge,
surrounded by silence on a seashore afternoon.

I never knew I loved to pray
at the altar of birdsong
after a cleansing rain,
sticky air,
sunspots on leaves.

I never knew I loved you—
Yes—I did—
but I never knew how to tell you
your voice is velvet caressing my skin.

LAMENT TO TIME

after Nâzim Hikmet

I never knew I loved each square inch of the familiar
'60s shag carpet, linoleum floors,
gas stove my father lit early in the morning
before he awakened me,
carried me
wrapped in my blanket to its warmth.
I can feel his arms and me, half-asleep,
resisting awakening.
I never knew how much I would miss those arms.

I never knew I'd miss cold
skating on frozen ponds,
ankles aching with teetering awkwardness,
red-tipped nose, body
encased in knit, wool,
white crunch of snow underfoot.

I never knew how much I loved blue-brown water of the Atlantic,
sticky sand in every crevice,
suntan-lotion sweat stinging my eyes.
I remember sunlight stinging my eyes:
lying on sand in fitful sleep
as voices fade farther, farther away.
Those voices now far far away.
I never knew I'd forget your voice.

I never knew I loved not knowing,
when the comfort of the unknown wrapped me in its embrace,
knowing still a gnat at the back of my eyes,
not yet engulfed in darkness.

HOLDING ON TO THE THINGS I LOVE

Sunlight sparkles rust leaves of the tree,
hanging on like things I love.
Rustling breeze feels like desire.
Gusts of longing burn my eyes;
reflections amaze.

You amaze.
Like birds resting in the branches of a tree,
a baby's sleepy eyes,
peace of things I love,
my heart's deep longing,
I settle in to dream my desire.

You are what I desire.
Your extraordinary charms amaze.
Birds fly to the objects of their longing
then return to safety of the tree.
I stretch my wings for love.
Love blinds my eyes.

A peacock has 100 eyes,
they say. Does each one desire
what they see? My eyes love
what I can't see. They amaze
me. I wonder if the tree
looks at robins with longing.

As expansive as the sky is my longing.
I dream things beyond my eyes.
Late-afternoon sun on leaves lights up the tree
in a spray of beauty, a desire

built on a serotonin-fueled fantasy, an amazing
fickleness, how much I want to love.

The setting sun, I love.
It disappears in a blaze of colors like my longing
for things I can't have. I'm amazed
at the view when fog lifts, the way my eyes
thought they saw desire.
The setting sun silhouettes the tree,

dusk's tree shadows dim. Love
looks as clear as cherry-tree blossoms blanketing the floor with
    longing.
When they disappear like remnants of a dream after you awake,
    they amaze.

MOTHER WOUND

Mother wound pierces deep,
manifests late-night ice-cream binges,
grasps at diamond castles in the sky.

Mother wound pierces deep
as Big Dipper, a container for longing as wide as the Andes,
as far away as a pilgrim harpist playing a whole-note Hallelujah
    on Mars.

Mother wound pierces deep,
dark, she's a raven crossing generations,
a parenthesis in time,

a sob in the back pocket of the softest jeans.
Mother wound pierces so deep
sometimes Cruella de Ville looks kind.

Mother Wound pierces a blind mouse,
strikes a clock three times,
drops a poison apple rotting from inside.

SEASON'S ROULETTE

In the time it takes to move from mammogram
to ultrasound to biopsy, late summer
turns to fall, once lush greens now crimsons, golds, browns, hold-
    ing on.

Now hold your breath, they say, *count one two
three*, a needle and numbing agent extract
a vision, they're reading tea leaves, searching for my fate,

a prophecy, waiting for the Tarot cards
to tell my future. Which cards will appear? I fear
the tumbling Tower. *It won't be painful,* a sting—

I feel a dozen hornets. Some women hide
their pain, I wear my anxiety like a gown.
How deep into my mind does the needle pierce?

Memories bleed. I see my father's lips.
Pursed. Labored. Breaths. He was 87
pounds when he died. Bedsores. Decomposing skin.

Hold on, they say, I grip the handle and see
age spots, then my mother's dying hands,
wrinkled sheets draping an unmade bed.

Now past tense, she's a late-night memory,
a ghostly reverie. I recall my sister's
mastectomy and wonder if my warranty

is up? I'm playing genetic lottery
with my family's history, waiting to see
if my winning numbers will be drawn,

wanting four and two girlfriends to stay with me,
sharing a vigil on this Shrine of Aging Ovaries,
four sleepless nights, four cartons of caramel gelato,

praying to the gods of medicine that
this time, I'll win. I read the horoscopes—my
liturgy— search for the Gospel of Good News.

I get a call but it's not news, it's time
to make my pagan sacrifice, the four-digit fee.
Finally, the Tarot Sun appears: a nurse's

voice with a casual tone; she's spun the wheel.
Death loses this round of Cancer Roulette but
leaves me with a reminder, a tiny heart-shaped scar

over my heart, the mother side, and a
marker in my breast which aches when it rains.
As if I were a cow, I'm tagged. Still, standing.

Outside, a Momiji leaf floats to the ground, crunches, rests.
A roly poly coils when stressed, rhododendrons
curl in the cold. Tulip bulbs burrow deep. We wait for spring.

WE ALWAYS WISH

We always wish for what we don't have,
a trumpet when what you have is a softly worn acoustic guitar;
a tangy mango instead of sweet smell of lavender underfoot.

We always wish for love,
twelve perfect princes,
white tigers accelerating toward earth,

stopping before the inevitable crash landing.
We always wish for a Monet moment,
field of tulips under a waxing moon,

well-arrayed, perfect as they are,
bitten by last night's frost
but king of the mountain to the bluebirds

dancing the broken Hallelujah.
We always wish for largest rooms,
open windows,

handsomest flowers,
nicest house,
when all that matters is a baby's deep breath.

THE MUTE PRINCESS

In my fantasy she took time for a swim,
she was a swan
until she found her voice.

She was not a quitter,
she was a multitasker,
committing leisure, work simultaneously,
birthing life, creativity,
suckling silence,
while we knew the impossible was yet to come.

She was extraordinarily charming,
with her wings bent like eaglets suddenly in flight
into a creamsicle periwinkle sunset.

She saw herself sweet as a bird's morning song
but could be fierce as a blue whale protecting her young.

She never measured,
always cut first,
her clock was correct two times a day.
In truth, she was a stuck accelerator circling earth,
she envied Snow White, her poison-apple sleep.

Sometimes we're swans,
sometimes we're geese,
sometimes we don't quite know what we are.

The woods.
The mute princess.
The mute king.
The mute sons.

We have mutated ourselves into carnivorous castles with secret
    rooms, passageways.
We have to get rid of evidence.
Forest animals know the signs.
A fox will chew off her own foot to escape a snare.
A fool skips blindly into a storm.

SHE

She couldn't help herself,
drawn to seven full moons
with a savior's complex as big as a sombrero.

She devoured need.
She once sailed to a country just bordering the forest,
scent of soap on fresh-washed skin lingering,

breasts budding,
to toil a labor of a serene-looking old woman.
She was mute, sad with no tears,

no one to wipe them away.
She wanted to save the world
but saving herself was harder work.

Wicked mother aside,
she did it all for the sake of a girl,
for the sake of a dream,

then watched it float away in a midsummer rain.

WITHOUT COMPROMISE

She lived like a seashell on a rocky shore,
tossed to and fro by frothy waves of fate.
A polyester soul, blend of courage, fear,
desire—stitched like a sneaker's ornate

sparkle, a footnote crucial to ignite
the plot. She rode sepia-toned landscapes
in the night, through the streets of Paris, bright;
she was a misunderstood, nondescript shape.

Her mood could warm you on a snowy day.
She had one foot in each world ready to fly.
She was looking glass, singer, she wanted to say
she wailed at full moons in a midnight sky.

She's finally singing her own morning song.
Now her mourning-song echo is where she belongs.

holy in Every Breath

IN THE BEGINNING § BLESS THE LOST
KINDNESSES § THIS I TRULY BELIEVE §
COMMITMENT

IN THE BEGINNING

I dreamed when Sophia,
goddess of Wisdom,
spoke the earth into being,

when she raised her great and powerful face to infinite blackness,
pin dots of stars began to form.
The harvest moon
illuminated earth,
white caps, angry waves
swirled around her feet.

Her toes sank in moist grit of sand,
she raised her arm heavenward—
the waters receded.
Alone,
a speck in the dry ocean bed,
seen from galaxies away.

Suddenly she spoke in a voice like a chanting monk.
At the sound I crawled from sea,
naked, shivering,
dragging the unexpected heaviness of my body.
I crawled on my belly,
slept from the effort of living.

When I awoke, she had left.
In her place, light of a thousand suns.
Where the waters had been,
a field of lush green
canopied under Yoshino cherry trees,
feathered blossoms,

breeze blowing sweet, light.
Scent of spring onions in unmown grass.

I watched a bee touch down on a petal,
hummingbird in blur,
fluorescent blues, greens,
mesmerizing grace, beauty,
faint buzzing; moving of air,
deep blue butterfly,
fluttering wings,
sunlight glancing.

I heard crickets crying.
Felt sun caressing my skin.

She saw everything and pronounced it very good.

I remembered sounds, smells
from my childhood.
My eyes opened to holy, mortal
merging as one,
harshness into my birth,
perpetual heaviness,
a light so bright it hurt to see.

I dreamed a vision in panoramic;
Sophia, gone.
I sobbed in despair,
my cries echoed
across the universe.

I dreamed I stood
on rocky ground,
feet bleeding,

blood sacrifice for a heart holding fast
in a world of darkness.

I was born in pain,
longing,
suffocating in a fine line between comfortable and stale,
in which everything, everyone
seems so far away,
memories fading
until shadows fill my sight.

BLESS THE LOST KINDNESSES

Holy source of love,
the world has lost her humanity, forgetting
community, generosity of heart.

Divine overcomer, miracle-maker, one who unites,
remind us,
bless us, transform lost kindnesses,
missing truths,
turn hatred into holiness;

lift up those left out, lying down, sitting down, standing down.

Let righteous indignation act courageously,
create a just world.

Show us a win, hope into action.

We speak for the voiceless.

May the overcomer of death overcome death
again
in our lifetime.

THIS I TRULY BELIEVE

The ceramic heart-shaped box with its baby blue painted-on
    doves lies silent,
the ashes hidden within,
inherent heaviness.

I believe the unnamed divine cries with us.
I believe presence overcomes decay, love, faith holding with
    breath.
I believe in silence, stillness, letting be.

I believe the holy paints me
one day at a time.

I believe in the shoot emerging from hidden seed.

May it be so.

COMMITMENT

I commit to radiate gold clouds exploding like July,
landing soft as a feather, warming your heart.
Radiate blue, true blue, solid as a rock, smooth as a stone,
leading a path from stability, order, wide as an ocean, heading
    home,
color of love, red, heart bleeding for those left behind.

I commit to radiate blue, true blue, solid as a rock, smooth as a
    stone,
orange, passion for justice, righteousness;
yellow, new day breaking forth,
color of love, red, heart bleeding for those left behind,
white for a purity that enfolds us all.

I commit to radiate orange, passion for justice, righteousness;
yellow, new day breaking forth,
leading a path from stability, order, wide as an ocean, heading
    home,
white for a purity that enfolds us all,
gold clouds exploding like July,
landing soft as a feather, warming your heart.

Ripening

THE CAREGIVER § TO THE BLACK FLY RESTING ON THE NURSING HOME TOILET § GRIEF: THE LONG GOODBYE § THE ESTATE SALE § THE RIPENING § "LA LUNA ES VIDA" § PRAISE BE § RITUAL TO RESTORE BEAUTY TO THE WORLD

THE CAREGIVER

incessant call

I need your help
I rang my bell
desperate, lonely

gray loon's lone wail

I rang my bell
I need your help
they won't come down

harsh winter's wind

diaper needs changed
I need I need
I tried to call

acrid crackling

I need I'm scared
please stay with me

gray sky streaks cry

I, I can't breathe
please don't hang up

shadows darken

help me I'm scared
stay stay with me

susurrations

I called I called
help, stay with me

inky blackness

I need come help
I tried to stand

time frozen, stilled

and then they left

snow falling soft

and then they left

fragrant winter
wildflowers

and then they left

fruited vine rot

TO THE BLACK FLY RESTING ON THE NURSING HOME TOILET

Black dot on white porcelain perch, small in vastness of time
    stretched middle
to end, to end, only body at home here, retching wretched bodies
    await,
only body knowing it will soar again. Amid sickness smells,
    moans, muffled,
bodies scattered, sitting in a muddle, feedlot cattle waiting, wait-
    ing for their fate.

Mouths perched like baby birds', waiting for their pills; and you,
    patiently waiting
for tumbling tiny crumbs dropped from their drooping lips, scat-
    tered in a puddle underfoot.
Your future: longer than the gray-haired lady's lying on the bed,
    time sedating;
you, the most alert one in this place. You, the only one not
    overlooked.

Black fly on the nursing home toilet resting, fixing your look, like
    a vulture
on the corporeal below, watching the sky for a sign, watching for
    death.
Loneliness caressing sleeping lying bodies praying for their
    rapture.
Loneliness possessing sleeping lying bodies dreaming of a peace-
    ful rest.

Remnants of months' old flowers lie scattered on the floor like
    lovers' tangled clothes.
Black fly, resting on a leaf, caressing petals of fading winter roses.

GRIEF: THE LONG GOODBYE

It's the only thing still clinging you to me.

Memories sold, yard sale cents on the dollar. Jeopardy
answers stay covered, their questions never asked.
Surrounded by ghosts. Cardinal incessantly tapping

the windowpane, ruby wings aflame,
shapeshifting from your heart to mine. They said
I needed boundaries. The day I set boundaries

was the day you died. I didn't know
needing me was keeping you alive. I
didn't know I built my home inside your need.

I tried to heal you through the force of my will.
I didn't know those were your own demons to fight.
Drinking from the cup of sadness, I toast you.

Distant birds chatter beneath the morning din.
We blew dandelion puffs across Nana's grave.
You have been floating away a long, long time.

THE ESTATE SALE

Your old record player lies hidden
behind the books,
family Bible,
vases curiously absent of dust,
porcelain figurines, Mary Magdalene and a green leprechaun,
Mom's collector Franklin Mint plates
worth nothing,
Aunt Mamie's hand-painted teacups,
pictures stuffed in boxes—
    friends and family, holidays and everydays, you and you and you
    rematerialized in Kodachrome—
boxes overflowing electronic cords and obsolete phone chargers,
blue whale bookmark I brought you from Hawaii,
green on green cork coasters from Ireland,
Dad's World War II Chinese chest holding the hand-me-down
    Raggedy Ann doll—cheeks painted with bright red lipstick—
    and a lock of your hair,
two large screen TVs,
two obsolete iPads,
overstuffed purple and orange easy chair,
electric recliner with automatic lift,
boxes of pill bottles,
pulse oximeter,
oxygen tank.

It was the record player,
unplayed for many years,
that made me miss you most.

THE RIPENING

The line between ripeness, decay is fine,
fruit, hard, green, suddenly lush, open,

juicy drips, soft, yielding until
one day
a press of your finger

pokes,
pierces,

a too-soft spot
mushy, new
rottenness forming,

you know the end is near.

Ripeness
hangs at eternity's edge.

"LA LUNA ES VIDA"

after Lorca

La luna brilla
para nosotros.
Nosotros vivimos
bajo la luna.

Nosotros vivimos
bajo las estrallas
y la noche
habla el silencio.

This silent night,
frost fills the air.
We prick the dark,
stardust, swirling by.

Pasan las estrallas
soñando con la luna
Flotan las estrallas
más allá de mi corazon.

The moon
shines for us.
We live
under the moon.

We live
under the stars
and the night
speaks silence.

This silent night,

frost fills the air.
We prick the dark,
stardust, swirling by.

The stars pass by
dreaming of the moon.
The stars float
beyond my heart.

PRAISE BE

Praise be to writing times carved out of cancellations.
To the word *no*. Warm sun emerges on a cloudy day.
Wind chimes ring. Unexpected old-friend invitations.
Adagio pauses. Ballerinas on display

who dance in music boxes tinkling *Tour de Lune*.
One hundred two reasons to stay. Prophets—Jeremiah
sings praises, cries the blues. Ezra Pound said *make it new*.
Write in praise of beautiful words—new Messiah.

Geologists study rocks. I study you. Peaches
plump and juicy sweet drip down my chin, sticky pleasure.
Words formed from magic scratches end up somewhere into
     flight,

they whirl. Remember, crickets near the edge float into night.
Wounds release their fears in summer's sweaty treasures.
Scorpion stings, sometimes scatters, sometimes simply teaches.

RITUAL TO RESTORE BEAUTY
TO THE WORLD

You must first wait for the tapping cardinal.
Sometimes she comes on a beam of sunlight.
Sometimes if you look closely, she is stardust.
Wander until you find a yellow daisy.
Cleanse yourself with a full moon's gathered rain.
Find one thing you haven't used in a year—discard.

Find one thought that is holding you back—discard.
Set out seed and secretly wait for the cardinal
to appear. Dance to call forth a little rain.
Open every curtain to let in sunlight.
Mix watercolor yellow, paint a daisy.
Lie on the ground at midnight, breathe in stardust.

Pirouette to Coppelia, breathe in stardust.
Find the narcissist in your address book—discard.
Lie on the ground and become a yellow daisy.
Sit in the sun and converse with the cardinal.
Put your face to the sky—bathe in sunlight.
Stand under a willow tree, wait for rain.

Notice the way the light sparkles on a leaf in the rain.
Notice the way the moon shimmers with stardust.
Notice the way silver blinds in sunlight.
Notice the dandelion weeds—do not discard,
for they are the favorite of the cardinal,
and she loves yellow flowers, like daisies.

She loves me, she loves me not, pick a daisy
gently, throw the petals into the rain.

Tell all your sorrows to the cardinal,
she will cleanse them, send them off on stardust.
Give her your saddest stories—she can discard.
Lie in the tall grass, feel the warmth of sunlight.

Put an amethyst crystal under sunlight.
Put a pearl on the head of a daisy.
Find the evil spell from last March—discard
(don't fret yourself about a little rain).
Remember, you are beautiful stardust,
this is known by everyone, even the cardinal.

The cardinal loves to come out in sunlight.
Sprinkle stardust on the nearest daisy.
Discard your umbrella, wait for rain.

ACKNOWLEDGEMENTS

I first want to thank Judyth Hill for her support and inspiration. Her guiding light, wisdom, and magic were invaluable to this collection of poems. Thank you to Mary Meade for the design work on this book and for playing with paintings with me.

I also want to acknowledge Christine Valters Painter, who rekindled in me a love of, and inspiration for, writing poetry, and Rusty Morrison, David Koehn, Jessica Jacobs, and Morrie Creech, from whom I've taken poetry classes and workshops.

Thank you to my poetry critique group who guided me through iterations of many of the poems in this book, always improving and encouraging: Barbara, Bruce, Diane, Doug, and Roman. Thank you to the Charlotte Center for Literary Arts and my Author's Lab friends and mentors: Justine, Mary, Neela, Melinda, Samantha, Emily, Grace, Molly, Paul, Heather, and Meg, for their encouragement and support of my writing.

Thank you to Robin and Jonah, for letting me use your stories, and to Robin for being the loving, kind person you are, and to Jonah, the best. Thank you to my Dad who made me a writer, and to Dad, Mom, Nana, Kelli, and Kathy for giving me a childhood to write about, through the good and the bad.

This collection is for Jerry for his unwavering support over many, many years, and for his love that inspires me every day.

PUBLICATION CREDITS

A Year of Magic: a previous version of this poem was published on Medium.com, 21 July 2017.

Another Wrinkle and White Hairs: a previous version of this poem was published on Medium.com, 27 June 2018.

Be Brave: a previous version of this poem was published on Medium.com, 11 March 2019.

Bless the Lost Kindnesses: a previous version of this poem was published on Medium.com, 6 July 2018.

Blessed Are the Broken: a previous version of this poem was published on Medium.com, 12 June 2017.

Courage: a previous version of this poem was published on Medium.com, 16 August 2017.

Dancing in the Dark: After Bill Holm's *Advice*.

Default to Life: a previous version of this poem was published on Medium.com, 6 August 2019.

Disappointing Plotlines: this poem was published in NC Bards, *Charlotte Poetry Anthology*, 2020.

Dreams: a previous version of this poem was published on Medium.com, 19 February 2019.

Eighth Day After the School Shooting: this poem was published in "After the School Shooting, in a Death Denying World," in *The Autoethnographer*, 29 May 2023.

Elegy for America: this poem was published in *Kakalak*, 2023.

Fifth Day After the School Shooting: this poem was published in "After the School Shooting, In a Death Denying World." In *The Autoethnographer*, 29 May 2023.

First Day After the School Shooting: this poem was published in "After the School Shooting, In a Death Denying World." In *The Autoethnographer*, 29 May 2023.

Honor: a previous version of this poem was published on Medium.com, 29 October 2017.

Hot Summer Sun: a previous version of this poem was published on Medium.com, 13 September 2018.

I Do Not Love You: After Neruda's *XVII Sonnet*

In the NICU: a previous version of this poem was published on Medium.com, 11 July 2017.

Is It a Secret if Everyone Knows It but No One Talks About It?: After Nâzim Hikmet's *Things I Didn't Know I Loved*

La Luna es Vida: After Lorca's *La Luna Asoma*

La Luna es Vida: this poem was published in *Stardust Review*, 2023.

Lament of Injustice: a previous version of this poem was published on Medium.com, 11 January 2018.

Lament to Evacuees: a previous version of this poem was published on Medium.com, 18 September 2018.

Lament to Time: After Nâzim Hikmet's *Things I Didn't Know I Loved*

Liminal Fear States: a previous version of this poem was published on Medium.com, 8 October 2018.

Losing the Weight: a previous version of this poem was published on Medium.com, 5 August 2017.

Lost Love Opportunities: a previous version was published on Medium.com, 3 March 2019.

Lying in Wait: this poem was published in *Penwood Review*, 2022.

Moonlight Sonnet: a previous version of this poem was published on Medium.com, 19 February 2019.

More: After Moya Cannon's *Inspiration*

Nana te Amo: a previous version of this poem was published on Medium.com, 29 May 2017.

Now You Reveal New Things to Me: a previous version of this poem was published on Medium.com, 30 May 2017.

On the Eve of Getting Test Results for My Best Friend: a previous version of this poem was published on Medium.com, 7 July 2017.

Ponderings: a previous version of this poem was published on Medium.com, 15 March 2019.

Ritual to Restore Beauty to the World: After Aborigine mother goddess Nungeena, Patricia Telesco (1998). *365 Goddess: A Daily Guide to the Magic and Inspiration of the Goddess.*

Season's Roulette: this poem was published in *Families, Systems, and Health*, 2022, 40(3), pp. 429-430.

Second Day After the School Shooting: this poem was published in "After the School Shooting, In a Death Denying World." In *The Autoethnographer*, 29 May 2023.

Shout Down These Walls: a previous version of this poem was published on Medium.com, 22 January 2019.

Start at the Heart: a previous version of this poem was published on Medium.com, 13 October 2017.

The NICU: a previous version of this poem was published on Medium.com, 31 May 2017.

Time Triggers: a previous version of this poem was published on Medium.com, 7 October 2018.

Welcome the Revolution: a previous version of this poem was published on Medium.com, 16 October 2017.

When: After Wendell Berry"s *The Peace of the Wild Things*

AUTHOR'S BIOGRAPHY

Christine Salkin Davis, PhD, is a writer, poet, and artist. A Fulbright Scholar and an Emeritus Professor of Communication Studies at UNC Charlotte, Davis writes poetry about her experiences with death and dying, spirituality, social justice, and compassionate living. Her poetry appears in her books exploring end of life communication in family, cultural, and political contexts, including: *Death: The Beginning of a Relationship* (Hampton Press, 2010), and *End of Life Communication: Stories from the Dead Zone* (with J. Crane, Routledge, 2019). Her poems have also been published in *Penwood Review, Moonstone Press* anthologies, *Kakalak*, and *Stardust Review*, among other publications. She is Nana to her grandson, and she loves to travel, hike, read, and practice ballet. She lives in Concord, North Carolina, with her husband, and her dog, Rumi. The poetry in this manuscript is an exploration of life, death, and the holy in the midst of life's messiness. For more information, please visit www.christinesalkindavis.com.

The body text of the passionate, tender poems in this collection is set in Adobe Caslon Pro, whose history in every way embodies the cri de coeur for social justice, for equal attention to the Infinite and the finite, heard in this poet's voice. This current version of the typeface, re-imagined by eclectic designer Carol Twombly, emerges from William Caslon's 1722 original punch cut type. Commissioned to create a typeface for an edition of the New Testament and influenced by the Dutch Baroque style then popular in London, Caslon created a new style of engraving type in the tradition of "old-style serif letter design," resembling handwritten letters. Used to set the original Declaration of Independence and the U.S. Constitution, this font's popularity inspired the expression, "When in doubt, use Caslon." The marvelous section openers are set in Lucida Blackletter. This font connects today's computer typography to the earliest printing in English: William Caxton used this style font in 1477 for the very first book printed in England. Renowned designers Charles Bigelow and Kris Holmes' lively interpretation of the cursive blackletter style, with its dark texture and fractured curves typical of the gothic type styles, is relaxed, playful, and exuberant, brilliantly supporting the poet's own unique, expressive watercolor updates of illuminated manuscript design. The titles, set in the modern font, Bebas Neue, designed by Ryoichi Tsunekawa, bridge time and style—being retro, classic, and contemporary—echoing the poet's fresh and vibrant use of traditional poetry forms.

www.ingramcontent.com/pod-product-compliance
Lightning Source LLC
Chambersburg PA
CBHW051636120626
46551CB00014B/2101